MW01610318

DEDICATION

We hope you enjoy the Los Angeles Dodgers Trivia Quiz Book.

CONTENTS

QUIZ 1

1. On April 18, 1958, The Dodgers baseball club, formerly from the Flatbush section of Brooklyn in New York, played their first game on the Pacific Coast as the Los Angeles Dodgers. What venue served as the site for the opening day game?
2. Which former Red Sox player wore the number 99 for the Dodgers in 2009?
3. Who was the manager of the 1963 and 1965 Los Angeles Dodgers championship teams?
4. Who was the manager of the LA Dodgers for the 2008 season?
5. The 1965 Dodgers were known for their strong pitching and weak offense. Their chances of winning the N.L. pennant appeared almost hopeless after their best offensive player suffered a season ending injury just 17 games into the season. Who broke his ankle and was lost for the season?
6. Who was the captain of the 1978 Dodgers?
7. Where did the Dodgers play before Los Angeles?
8. In the early and mid-fifties, choose the primary broadcasters used for the TV games.
9. In 1888, in the very city where the legendary Candy Cummings had invented the curveball, there were seven weddings, weddings that would loom large in one of sports most storied franchises. For in 1890, these seven relative newlywed men and their team would leave the less highly regarded American Association to join the National League. Under what name did this team that would ultimately become the Dodgers play in 1890?
10. Who did the Dodgers play in the first regular season home game at Ebbets Field?

ANSWERS QUIZ 1

1. Los Angeles Coliseum

2. Manny Ramirez

3. Walter Alston

4. Joe Torre

5. Tommy Davis

6. Davey Lopes

7. Brooklyn

8. Red Barber, Connie Desmond, Vin Scully, Andre Baruch

9. The Brooklyn Bridegrooms

10. Philadelphia Phillies

QUIZ 2

1. Before they played in the 1959 World Series, the Dodgers had to defeat what team, as they finished tied for 1st in the National League?
2. The Dodgers moved to Los Angeles to play in the 1958 season. Where were they located before?
3. In Dodger history, which of the following team names were they NEVER called?
4. When right fielder, Shawn Green, broke the Dodgers franchise record, in 2001, for most homeruns in a season, whose record did he beat?
5. Who was the first player for the Dodgers franchise to win the NL MVP award?
6. What did Babe Herman do for the first time (of a major league record 3 times) on May 18, 1931?
7. Who was the owner of the Dodgers that spearheaded the move of the team from Brooklyn to Los Angeles?
8. Dodger Stadium is located in which Los Angeles park?
9. The Los Angeles Dodgers won the 1963 National League pennant with a record of 99-63. Which team led by Ken Boyer, finished second to the Dodgers in 1963?
10. Which player saw opening day starting shortstop duties for the LA Dodgers?

ANSWERS QUIZ 2

1. Milwaukee Braves
2. Brooklyn
3. Browns
4. Gary Sheffield
5. Dolph Camilli
6. Hit for the cycle
7. Walter F. O'Malley
8. Elysian Park
9. St. Louis Cardinals
10. Rafael Furcal

QUIZ 3

1. The Dodgers lost their best hitter for the season due to a broken ankle just two weeks into the season. Who was the journeyman player they called up from the minors to take his place?

2. With nagging injuries and off years by Rick Monday and Glen Burke, center field proved to be a weakness for the 1978 Dodgers. Whom did they acquire midway through the season to play center field and try to shore up this weakness?

3. What team was not in the Dodgers division in 2006?

4. On what channel were the Dodger games broadcast in New York?

5. In 1911, the team adopted a new name, a name that reflected life in American cities in the early 20th century. What kind of "dodgers" did the team become in 1911?

6. If a player hit the Abe Stark sign in right field, what did he win?

7. What Dodger set a World Series record when he hit two pinch hit home runs in the 1959 World Series?

8. What manager transitioned the team from Brooklyn to Los Angeles?

9. What Dodger of the 20th Century has the highest career strikeout ratio per nine innings pitched with at least two full seasons with the Dodgers?

10. Glenn Hoffman, the brother of the San Diego Padres' All-Star closer, Trevor Hoffman, was a coach from 1999 to 2005 for the Dodgers. Which position did he coach?

ANSWERS QUIZ 3

1. Lou Johnson
2. Bill North
3. New York Yankees
4. Ch. 9
5. The Trolley Dodgers
6. suit
7. Chuck Essegian
8. Walter Alston
9. Hideo Nomo
10. Third Base

QUIZ 4

1. The Dodgers franchise retired the number 19 in my honor. Who am I?
2. For how many seasons did Walter Alston manage the Dodgers?
3. From the first Dodgers' game played in Los Angeles (1958), until the end of the 2008 season (50 years later), who managed the team for the most number of full seasons?
4. Which former Brooklyn Dodger had his number retired throughout the Major Leagues in 1997?
5. Sandy Koufax was a dominant pitcher for the Los Angeles Dodgers in 1963 and again in 1965. Which uniform number did this superstar wear?
6. What Boston Red Sox outfielder did the Dodgers acquire in a July 2008 trade?
7. The pitching staff was anchored by Hall of Famers Sandy Koufax and Don Drysdale. How many games did they combine to win in 1965?
8. The 1977 Dodgers were the first team to have four players hit 30 or more home runs in a season. How many Dodgers hit 30 or more in 1978?
9. Which of the following stadiums did the franchise play their home games for the least amount of time?
10. What was the name of the pre-game show, aimed at the kids, and appearing before every home game?

ANSWERS QUIZ 4

1. Jim Gilliam
2. 23
3. Tommy Lasorda
4. Jackie Robinson
5. 32
6. Manny Ramirez
7. 49
8. 0
9. Los Angeles Memorial Coliseum
10. Happy Feltons' Knothole Gang

QUIZ 5

1. In 1934, the Giant's manager was asked about the Brooklyn Dodger's prospects and replied, "Haven't heard a peep from there, is Brooklyn still in the league?" This insult is credited with triggering all of the following except for what?
2. Who was the umpire that was attacked on the field at Ebbets Field in 1940?
3. What player was named MVP of the 1959 World Series, after winning 2 games and saving 2 games.
4. When did the Los Angeles Dodgers win their first World Series?
5. How many career wins did Sandy Koufax retire with?
6. Who was the last Dodger to make it into the 30-30 club in the 1990s, with at least 30 homeruns and 30 stolen bases in the same season?
7. In 1994 I was voted the top Rookie in the National League. Who am I?
8. Who was the first NL Player to win MVP and Cy Young awards in the same season?
9. Between 1958 and 2008, which American League team did NOT face the Los Angeles Dodgers in post season World Series Play?
10. Who are the Dodgers' halo-wearing crosstown rivals?

ANSWERS QUIZ 5

1. The Dodgers winning a pennant

2. George Magerkurth

3. Larry Sherry

4. 1959

5. 165

6. Raul Mondesi

7. Raul Mondesi

8. Don Newcombe

9. Kansas City Athletics

10. Angels

QUIZ 6

1. Which one of these Los Angeles players, a centerfielder, did not hit a home run against the New York Yankees in the 1963 World Series?
2. What Dodger struck out over 150 times during the 2008 season?
3. Who was the Dodgers' third starter behind Koufax and Drysdale who chipped in 15 wins in 1965?
4. The Dodgers and Reds had a great rivalry in the 1970s, as they accounted for 9 of the 10 N.L. West titles in the decade. But another team was also in contention for the division title in 1978. Which team?
5. What two letters are used on the hat as the logo for the Los Angeles Dodgers?
6. One of the announcers was plucked directly from Fordham University without previous professional experience, and became a famous play-by-play star later in his career. Who was this?
7. In 1937, the Dodgers received their unofficial nickname of "bums". Very appropriately, a cabby inspired this turn of events when he inquired of his passenger, "So how did those bums do today?" What was the occupation of the passenger, Willard Mullin, who was responsible for publicizing the name "bums"?
8. Who was the only Dodgers' player to hit four home runs in a single game at Ebbets Field?
9. Who did Sandy Koufax whiff for his World Series record 15th strike out, in game 1 of the 1963 World Series?
10. Who was the first Los Angeles Dodger to hit 40 home runs in a season?

ANSWERS QUIZ 6

1. Willie Davis

2. Matt Kemp

3. Claude Osteen

4. Giants

5. LA

6. Vince Scully

7. Sports cartoonist

8. Gil Hodges

9. Harry Bright

10. Mike Piazza

QUIZ 7

1. What 20th Century Dodger has the highest single-season batting average?

2. Which Dodger pitcher led the National League with the lowest ERA (Earned Run Average) in 2000?

3. Which one of these players had the most RBIs in a single season for the Dodgers?

4. When did the Dodgers play their first game in Los Angeles?

5. The Los Angeles Dodgers has always been known for their strong pitching staff. From 1958 through 2008, which team pitcher recorded the most victories?

6. There was a blue sign on the hills outside on the north side of Dodger Stadium for many years. What did the famous sign say?

7. Which speedy switch-hitter was the starting shortstop for the 1963 and 1965 Los Angeles Dodgers?

8. Which Dodger starting pitcher finished the 2008 season with a disappointing 6.27 ERA?

9. Who was the rookie second baseman that tied for the team lead in home runs and won the N.L. Rookie of the Year award?

10. The Dodgers were in 3rd place when they called up a young pitcher in late June. Filling both starting and relief roles, this pitcher won 7 games, saved 3 and posted a 2.02 ERA as the Dodgers eventually took over first place in mid August. Who was this pitcher?

ANSWERS QUIZ 7

1. Babe Herman

2. Kevin Brown

3. Tommy Davis

4. 18-Apr-58

5. Don Sutton

6. Think Blue

7. Maury Wills

8. Brad Penny

9. Jim Lefebvre

10. Bob Welch

QUIZ 8

1. What are the main colors for the Los Angeles Dodgers?

2. What was the name of the street into which Duke Snider would hit most of his "homers", a fairly long and well-known Brooklyn thoroughfare?

3. In 1937, the Dodgers finished 33 games out of first place. Some might say that it was with the hiring of a new manager in 1939 that the bums of summer became "The Boys of Summer". Who was hired to manage the Dodgers in 1939 (Hint: he later became a third base coach for the team)?

4. Where in Ebbets Field did Hilda Chester sit with her infamous cowbell?

5. What Dodgers' 3-run homer proved to be the difference in their 5-2 victory, in game 1 of the 1963 World Series?

6. Where did the Dodgers play their home games upon moving to Los Angeles?

7. Which of the following Dodgers has NOT hit over 300 career doubles?

8. During the 2001 season _____ Lo Duca played as a Dodger catcher, 1st baseman, and left fielder.

9. Who was the first Dodgers player to win concecutive NL batting titles?

10. Who was the 'Rookie of the Year' in 1979?

ANSWERS QUIZ 8

1. Blue and white

2. Bedford Avenue

3. Leo Durocher

4. left center field bleachers

5. John Roseboro

6. Los Angeles Memorial Coliseum

7. Gil Hodges

8. Paul

9. Jake Daubert

10. Rick Sutcliffe

QUIZ 9

1. Since opening day at Dodger Stadium in 1962, Bob Mitchell, Chauncey Haines, Don Beamsley, Helen Dell, and Nancy Bea Hefley have (at different times) worked in a stadium position that enhanced the overall Dodgers' experience for millions of fans and visitors attending home games. What job title did they share?

2. This man is a historic sportscaster. He broadcasted the Dodger games in addition to many other sporting events for over 50 years. Who is this icon?

3. In 1965, the Los Angeles Dodgers lost the first two games of the World Series to the Minnesota Twins. Which Dodgers' lefty starter, number 23, won game three for L.A.?

4. Which outfielder led the 2008 Dodgers in home runs?

5. Which of the following feats were the 1965 Dodgers, the first team in Major League baseball history to accomplish?

6. Another incident is credited with awakening the Dodgers from their lackluster play. After this happened, they went 21-11 and turned a 1 game lead into a 7 1/2 game lead with 7 to play. What happened?

7. Who was the first African-American player to play for the Dodgers?

8. This Brooklyn manager never wore a uniform. He did his business in a business suit. Who was it?

9. The year 1947 was a banner year for the Dodgers, easing some of the futility of the previous 25 years in which they had won only two pennants and not one World Series. Which of the following did the Dodgers do in 1947?

ANSWERS QUIZ 9

1. In-House Stadium Musician

2. Vin Scully

3. Claude Osteen

4. Andre Ethier

5. They had an all switch-hitting infield

6. A clubhouse fight between Don Sutton and Steve Garvey

7. Jackie Robinson

8. Burt Shotton

9. All these

QUIZ 10

1. What special event took place at Ebbets Field during the game between the Dodgers and Cardinals on August 2, 1938.

2. Sandy Koufax won two games in the 1963 World Series, and set a single game strikeout record with 15 in game 1. But the best pitched game of the series may have been in game 3 when what pitcher allowed only 3 hits, struck out 9 and walked none, in a 1-0 Dodger win?

3. In what year did the Los Angeles Dodgers first win 100 games in a season?

4. Which of the following Dodgers has more career shutouts?

5. During the 2001 regular season, which Dodger pitcher only pitched with Chad Krueter catching?

6. Which was the last year the Dodgers franchise won the NL pennant in the 20th century?

7. Who hit the 7,000th home run in Dodger history?

8. Primarily known for their pitching, the Los Angeles Dodgers produced a number of fine hitters in their first five decades as well. During those 50 years, which Los Angeles Dodgers slugging star has been responsible for the most home runs?

9. Dodger Jim Lefebvre wore the number 5 for the Dodgers in addition to many other greats. Which former Astros and Padres player wore the number 5 in the 2009 season?

10. This L.A. Dodgers player, a left-handed right fielder, led the club with 11 base hits against the Twins in the 1965 World Series. Can you identify this player who wore uniform number 6?

ANSWERS QUIZ 10

1. yellow baseballs used

2. Don Drysdale

3. 1962

4. Don Drysdale

5. Chan Ho Park

6. 1988

7. Reggie Smith

8. Eric Karros

9. Mark Loretta

10. Ron Fairly

QUIZ 11

1. What team did LA trade with to re-acquire Greg Maddux in 2008?

2. On September 9, Sandy Koufax pitched a perfect game in beating the Cubs 1-0. The Dodgers themselves got only one hit. Who was the Cubs' pitcher who threw a one-hitter and lost?

3. Which pitcher led the Dodgers in wins in 1978?

4. What were the Dodgers called before the "Dodgers"?

5. Who became the Dodgers version of Mariano Rivera because he was a practically lights out closer and one of the first great relievers?

6. On August 11, 1951, the Dodgers led the National league by 13 games. However, when the season ended they found themselves tied and in a three-game playoff with the Giants. Ahead 4-1 in the bottom of the ninth, how did Dodger reliever Ralph Branca end the inning?

7. Casey Stengel was famous in Ebbets Field lore for the time he doffed his cap before his at-bat, and a bird flew out from under the cap. What team was Stengel playing for at the time?

8. In 1965, Sandy Koufax did not pitch game 1 in observance of Yom Kippur, a Jewish holiday. Who started in his place and didn't last through the 3rd inning in an 8-2 Dodger loss?

9. Who was the first Los Angeles Dodger pitcher to win 25 games in a season?

10. In history, how many Dodger players have hit 300 or more career home runs?

ANSWERS QUIZ 11

1. San Diego Padres

2. Bob Hendley

3. Burt Hooton

4. The Robins

5. Clem Labine

6. By giving up a game-winning home run to Bobby Thomson

7. Pittsburgh Pirates

8. Don Drysdale

9. Don Drysdale

10. 2

QUIZ 12

1. When did the Brooklyn Dodgers become the Los Angeles Dodgers?

2. Who was the last Dodger player to win the NL MVP award in the 20th century?

3. What year did Chan Ho Park make his major league debut?

4. The first 50 years, 1958 to 2008- during those 50 years the organization produced twelve "Rookie of the Year" players, the most for any major league team during that time frame. Which Los Angeles Dodgers' player was NOT named a season Rookie of the Year?

5. The Dodgers in 2009 went through the season with a four-man starting rotation for pitching. Winning the National League West Division, the team's winningest pitcher won how many games in the season?

6. Jim Gilliam was a veteran, versatile infielder who played on the 1963 and 1965 L.A. Dodgers' World Series champion teams. What was his nickname?

7. Which Dodger led the 2008 roster in RBIs?

8. The 1965 National League pennant race was a thriller, with 6 teams within 5 1/2 games of first place on September 1. In September, the Dodgers went on a winning streak to ultimately win the N.L. pennant by 2 games. How long was this game-winning streak?

ANSWERS QUIZ 12

1. 1958

2. Kirk Gibson

3. 1994

4. Maury Wills

5. 12

6. Junior

7. James Loney

8. 13

QUIZ 13

1. In game 4 of the National League Championship Series vs. the Phillies, which Philadelphia outfielder dropped a fly ball in the bottom of the 10th inning that ultimately helped the Dodgers score a run and win the pennant?

2. What number did the legendary pitcher Sandy Koufax wear for the Dodgers?

3. What famous Brooklyn park was Ebbets Field next to?

4. Walter O'Malley had become the controlling owner and team president in 1950. In 1954, he shocked many when he hired "Walter Who" to manage the team. What was the last name of this "quiet man" with whom Walter O'Malley would sign 23 consecutive one-year contracts?

5. How many All-Star Games were played at Ebbets Field?

6. The Twins appeared to be in good shape after beating beating Sandy Koufax in game 2 of the 1965 Series, as they headed to L.A with a 2-0 series lead. Who tossed a complete game, 5-hit shutout to get the Dodgers back in the series?

7. Which of the following Los Angeles Dodgers, had more victories in a Dodger uniform?

8. How many Dodgers of the 20th Century won 27 or more games in a season?

9. For five consecutive season from 1992 to 1996, a Dodger received the N.L. Rookie of the Year Award. What is the order in which they received them?

10. In my career as a member of the Dodgers franchise I had 335 stolen bases. Who am I?

ANSWERS QUIZ 13

1. Garry Maddox

2. 32

3. Prospect Park

4. Alston

5. one

6. Claude Osteen

7. Don Sutton

8. 3

9. Karros, Piazza, Mondesi, Nomo, Hollandsworth

10. Willie Davis

QUIZ 14

1. What year did the Dodgers begin their long association with Vero Beach as their training home?

2. What distinction do former Los Angeles Dodgers' players Frank Robinson, Dusty Baker, Jeff Torborg, and Mike Scioscia share?

3. Which 2006 player along with Eric Gagne, became the first French-Canadian battery in Major League Baseball?

4. In the 1965 World Series, which Minnesota right-handed starter nicknamed "Mudcat", defeated the L.A. Dodgers twice?

5. Which 2008 Dodger starting pitcher had the lowest ERA at 3.14?

6. Among players with at least 75 at-bats, who led the 1965 Dodgers in both batting average and slugging percentage?

7. The Dodgers' joy at winning their second straight N.L. title turned to sorrow the next day as their popular 1st base coach and former player died tragically at age 50 of a cerebral hemmorage. Who?

8. Which of these players never played for the Dodgers?

9. What stood where Ebbets Field was today?

10. As the 1955 season began, the Yankees had won 16 World Series, the Giants five, the Dodgers zero. Which of the following events occurred in this landmark season?

ANSWERS QUIZ 14

1. 1948

2. Voted a league " Manager of the Year"

3. Russell Martin

4. Jim Grant

5. Chad Billingsley

6. Don Drysdale

7. Jim Gilliam

8. Satchel Paige

9. A housing project

10. All these

QUIZ 15

1. In what city did the Dodgers play 15 home games in 1956 and 1957?

2. Who hit a solo homer off the left field foul pole in game 7 of the 1965 Series, to give Sandy Koufax the only run he needed as the Dodgers won the series?

3. What Los Angeles Dodger set a team record for highest batting average in a season by hitting .362?

4. In Jackie Robinson's Dodger career, how many times was he hit by a pitch?

5. When did the Dodgers receive the NL Wild Card for the first time?

6. Which of these Dodger pitchers led the NL in strikeouts for seven concecutive seasons?

7. Which Dodger struck out Reggie Jackson on an unforgettable moment in Game 2 of the 1978 World Series?

8. Working as a baseball scout, a coach, a manager, and a front office executive, Tommy Lasorda was one of two people to have spent 50 years in the Los Angeles Dodgers' organization. What was the job title of the other person?

9. The 2009 Dodger roster saw only one batter hit over .300 who played in at least 100 games. Who was he?

10. Wes Parker, number 28, was the starting first baseman for the 1965 Los Angeles Dodgers. Which one of these statements about Parker is true?

ANSWERS QUIZ 15

1. Jersey City

2. Lou Johnson

3. Mike Piazza

4. 72

5. 1996

6. Dazzy Vance

7. Bob Welch

8. Play by play announcer

9. Juan Pierre

10. He was a switch-hitter who threw left-handed

QUIZ 16

1. What was the outcome of the 2008 LA Dodger season?

2. The highlight for the Dodgers in the World Series was in game 2 when Bob Welch struck out Reggie Jackson in the 9th inning to save the Dodgers 4-3 win and give them a 2-0 Series lead. What was the situation when Jackson struck out?

3. Which one of these years was not a year when the Dodgers won a World Series?

4. Which Brooklyn Dodger won the first Cy Young award?

5. Even the best exertions of the mighty O'Malley, he could not secure for our beloved Dodger heroes, the stadium they so richly deserved in Brooklyn. Even after the Dodgers vanquished their nemesis the Yankees in the World Series, even when shown plans for baseball's first domed stadium, the powerful Lords of Brooklyn remained intent on keeping our boys imprisoned in dilapidated Ebbet's Field. But on May 2, 1957, flying in a police helicopter through the sunny Southern California skies, the astute O'Malley descried the key to his team's future, Chavez Ravine. According to his online biography, which feature of the geography did Walter O'Malley find particularly impressive?

6. Who did the Dodgers play in their last home game at Ebbets Field?

7. In game 2 of the 1966 Series, this normally sure handed fielder made 3 errors in one inning, leading to 3 unearned Oriole runs in their 6-0 victory. Who was the player?

8. Who was the first Los Angeles Dodger starter, to hit over .300 in a season?

ANSWERS QUIZ 16

1. National League Division Champions

2. Men on first and second

3. 1973

4. Don Newcombe

5. A confluence of freeways to bring fans to the park

6. Pittsburgh Pirates

7. Willie Davis

8. Duke Snider

QUIZ 17

1. Which of the following was NEVER a Dodger manager?

2. Who had the most triples in the 2001 regular season as a Dodger?

3. In my career as a member of the Dodgers franchise I had 2804 hits. Who am I?

4. What Major League record did Manny Mota set on September 2, 1979?

5. The Dodgers' brilliant starting pitchers had a league-leading 58 complete games, but occasionally needed help from the bullpen. Who led the Dodgers in saves in 1965?

6. In the 9th inning of game 2 of the 1974 Series, the Dodgers were clinging to a 3-2 lead, when reliever Mike Marshall picked what Oakland runner off first base to stop a potential rally?

7. How many strike outs did Ramon Martinez have against the Atlantia Braves in a 6-0 win on June 4, 1990?

8. Why didn't Sandy Koufax pitch game one of the 1965 World Series?

9. In game 5 of the 1974 Series, the Dodgers were facing elimination and trailed 3-2 in the 8th inning. Which player led off the inning by being thrown out trying to stretch a double into a triple?

10. Against which team did Hideo Nomo get his first major league win?

ANSWERS QUIZ 17

1. Mark Ward

2. Tom Goodwin

3. Zack Wheat

4. career pinch hits

5. Ron Perranoski

6. Herb Washington

7. 18

8. Game 1 fell on Yom Kippur, Judaism's holiest day

9. Bill Buckner

10. New York Mets

QUIZ 18

1. The Twins stunned the Dodgers by winning games one and two of the World Series, beating ace pitchers Drysdale and Koufax in the process. Who helped the Dodgers get back in the series by pitching a five-hit shutout in game three?

2. Which year was the All Star Game played at Dodger Stadium?

3. Who hit a home run off the left field foul pole in the 4th inning of game 7, breaking a scoreless tie as the Dodgers won, 2-0.

4. Who was the MVP of the 1977 World Series?

5. Against which team did Sandy Koufax pitch a perfect game on September 9, 1965?

6. Sandy Koufax was 26-8 with a 2.04 ERA, and he set the single season strikeout record with 382. However, he finished 2nd in N.L. MVP voting. Who was the 1965 N.L. MVP?

7. When Bob Welch dramatically struck out Reggie Jackson in the 9th inning of game 2 of the 1978 World Series, who was the Dodgers' winning pitcher?

ANSWERS QUIZ 18

1. Claude Osteen

2. 1980

3. Lou Johnson

4. Reggie Jackson

5. Chicago Cubs

6. Willie Mays

7. Burt Hooton

QUIZ 19

1. Who did the Sporting News name as the first ever 'Rookie of the Year' on September 12, 1947?

2. In game 4 of the 1981 World Series, this Dodger's clutch pinch hit 2-run homer ignited a rally that saw L.A. overcome a 6-3 deficit, in an 8-7 victory that evened the series at 2-2. Who was the player?

3. Yankee relief pitcher George Frazier set a record by losing 3 games in the 1981 World Series. Who was the other Yankee pitcher who took a loss in this Series that was won by L.A. 4 games to 2?

4. While Reggie Jackson was known as "Mr. October", because of his post season heroics, Yankee owner George Steinbrenner dubbed this player, "Mr. May" after he batted .045 with only 1 RBI in the 1981 Series. Who was the player?

5. What former Oakland A's player had a big role in the Dodger's 1988 series victory, as he was on base when Gibson homered in game 1, and he homered himself in the game 5 clincher?

ANSWERS QUIZ 19

1. Jackie Robinson

2. Jay Johnstone

3. Ron Guidry

4. Dave Winfield

5. Mike Davis

Made in the USA
Las Vegas, NV
15 June 2021